Mark Shelton is a freelance legal trainer, having practised in major commercial law firms for thirty years. He qualified with Linklaters and has always specialised in property litigation. Mark was a Partner at Lawrence Graham, and has acted for major property investors, financial institutions and leading retailers. He was a Professional Support Lawyer for a number of years, most recently at Eversheds Sutherland LLP, working with the UK's largest specialist real estate litigation team. He is a contributor to Estates Gazette, Property Week and Property Law Journal, the author of The Lease Guide website, and the author of books on Dilapidations; Landlord's Consents; Forfeiture of Leases.

Covid-19, Brexit and the Law of Commercial Leases – The Essential Guide

Covid-19, Brexit and the Law of Commercial Leases – The Essential Guide

Mark Shelton

MA (Hons) Law (Cantab), Non-Practising Solicitor

Commercial Property Management Law Trainer

Author of The Lease Guide website

www.marksheltontraining.co.uk

www.theleaseguide.co.uk

Law Brief Publishing

Published 2020 by Law Brief Publishing, an imprint of Law Brief Publishing Ltd
30 The Parks
Minehead
Somerset
TA24 8BT

www.lawbriefpublishing.com

Paperback: 978-1-913715-04-5

Dedicated to the other published Sheltons,

my father John and brother Rick

PREFACE

It is a trite observation that business hates uncertainty, but over the four years since the EU referendum vote, it has had to cope with little else, at unprecedented levels, and in relation to entirely novel issues. Nor is the end in sight.

The Covid-19 pandemic will come to an end, and of course one hopes that it will be sooner rather than later, but caution will probably dictate that aspects of the lockdown, and other restrictions on normal life and commercial activity, will continue for some time thereafter into a 'lock-down hangover'. While opinions differ as to the likely economic impact of the pandemic and the lockdown (and of course the impact is global as well as national), it is universally accepted that it will be major, and that the period of recovery will be of uncertain duration.

Thrown into the mix is the final outcome of the Brexit process. Any extension of the transition period provided for in the Withdrawal Agreement would have to be agreed by 30 June 2020, less than three weeks away at the time of writing, and it presently seems unlikely that there will be one. In the absence of any extension, the period will come to an end at 11.00 pm on 31 December 2020, at which time Britain will have full third-party status as regards the EU, and will cease to be a member of the single market and the customs union. There is, of course, a range of different views as to what effect this will have upon business and the economy, but no predictions can be made with any confidence until it is known what, if any, deal will be agreed between the UK and the EU.

Covid-19 and Brexit are being considered together in this book because the fact that both events have coincided cannot be ignored, and the likely implications of each for future leases have much in common. Commercial leases, while being granted for comparatively short terms in present market conditions, nevertheless represent commitments which will endure over, usually, several years. A prolonged period of economic uncertainty dictates that lease provisions must attempt, more than usual, to allow for change, though landlord and tenant will naturally have competing objectives, and what can be agreed will depend upon strength of bargaining positions.

As well as having implications for future leases, the Covid-19 episode has caused problems for the implementation of existing lease arrangements. Government has responded to the crisis by imposing restrictions upon the measures available for the recovery of rent and other sums due under leases. The result has been that many landlords and tenants have been entering into concession agreements of one sort or another. The nature of those concessions may or may not tell us something about what tenants will be looking for in new leases, but in any event concession agreements present some difficulties and pitfalls in themselves. This book will also address those issues.

The book has been written while the history of these events is itself being written. The likely shape of Brexit will appear in coming weeks, as will the nature and pace of Britain's emergence from lockdown. The situation changes almost daily, so that some of the contents will inevitably become out of date fairly quickly. Nevertheless, just as businesses cannot wait for years before taking decisions on commercial leases, neither can advisers wait for years before assisting in those decisions, so it is hoped that this snapshot of the present situation will nevertheless have a practical use.

The law is stated as at 12 June 2020.

Mark Shelton
June 2020

CONTENTS

CHAPTER ONE
LEASES IN UNCERTAIN TIMES –
IDENTIFYING THE ISSUES

Covid-19

The impact of the Covid-19 pandemic and associated lockdown upon the commercial property world has been sudden, dramatic and wide-ranging, and what the landscape will look like in, say, two years' time, is impossible to know.

The retail, leisure and hospitality sectors were hit by a wave of voluntary closures prior to the lockdown, and have since been almost completely closed down by government action. All retailers other than those identified as essential were required to close under the *Coronavirus Act 2020*. Local Data Company has estimated that 69% of all retail premises in the UK are non-essential; taking into account stores which, though falling into the essential list, closed voluntarily, around 83% of retail stock has been closed down. At the date of writing, garden centres, car showrooms and open-air markets have recently been permitted to re-open, other non-essential retailers will be permitted to re-open from 15 June, and the government hopes to allow more businesses to re-open in coming weeks, though social distancing, staff shortages and hygiene requirements will affect the operation of shops, restaurants, hotels and others.

Of those workplaces not required to close by government action, many have been closed voluntarily anyway as a precaution. Some office occupiers have chosen to remain open, though with many staff furloughed or working from home; while many factories have continued to function with adjustments to working methods and hygiene arrangements. The logistics sector has been crucial to the continued functioning of the economy, and logistics sites have remained open. Some businesses which closed voluntarily are now re-opening, though for them, as well as for those which never closed, social distancing requirements and staff shortages may limit their operation.

The effect upon business has necessarily been severe, though not uniformly so. Grocery sales have seen significant increase, as have sales of computers, office equipment and bicycles, but other non-food retail has suffered badly. Indications are that only a small proportion of the sales which would have been made in-store have transferred to online. The supply chain infrastructure which might enable that is insufficient, and many retailers have suspended online sales out of consideration for the safety of warehouse staff. High-profile insolvencies on the high street so far include Carluccio's, Cath Kidston, Debenhams, Warehouse, Oasis, Frankie & Benny's, Monsoon and Accessorize, and more may be expected.

Both landlords and tenants will be anxious over the sustainability of tenants' businesses. Dealing with rental liabilities and funding the provision of services are obvious headaches, but one thing is plain: a landlord and tenant relationship which is administered in all respects in accordance with the lease terms is likely to be the exception rather than the rule, for some time to come. The obligations in leases may now appear to both sides as obstacles to be side-stepped, or hurdles to be overcome, rather than matters for enforcement come what may. Certain landlords may be subject to superior lease obligations or banking covenants which require them to enforce occupational tenant's obligations, but it is equally unlikely that those covenants will be insisted upon.

In the interests of long-term stability, sustainability of businesses and protecting investments, many landlords and tenants are working together to find ways through the crisis. Intu has supported occupiers with an 11% reduction in its service charge budget for the year; British Land, Network Rail, TfL and Gentian have delayed or cancelled rents due on 25 March 2020, and many more landlords are agreeing concessionary arrangements with their tenants to help them survive the crisis.

On the other hand, ukactive, representing gyms and leisure centres, has reported a growing number of cases of landlords seeking to enforce payment of rent by the use of commercial rent arrears recovery (CRAR), court proceedings, or statutory demands and insolvency proceedings. Government has responded with a number of restrictions on the exercise of the available rent recovery methods.

Brexit

The Covid-19 pandemic and accompanying lockdown have understandably dominated news and commentary for the past two months and more, and Brexit may feel like yesterday's issue. But the deadline is still approaching, and so far the British government has resisted arguments for an extension of the transition period, whether prompted by the impact of Covid-19 or otherwise. At the time of writing, the United Kingdom is due, on 31 December 2020, to cease to be part of the EU single market and customs union.

Whether this picture will change should become clearer very shortly, since any extension of the transition period must be agreed by 1 July 2020. The EU's position to date is that any wider free trade deal is dependent upon agreement being reached on future fishing arrangements, and that that must occur by 1 July in order to agree any extension. No deal on fisheries appears likely. In any event, the British government presently maintains that whether or not there is an agreement on fisheries by 1 July, no extension will be agreed.

As things stand, it appears a real possibility that the UK and EU will not achieve a free trade deal by 31 December, and that from 1 January 2021 our trading relationship will be governed by World Trade Organisation rules. That means cross-border movement of goods would be subject to customs checks, and not, therefore, 'frictionless'. Tariffs would be payable at WTO levels, which may lead to a loss of competitiveness. Immigration into the UK would be a matter of British government policy, and the EU's principle of free movement of people would no longer apply.

It would be what has been variously referred to as a 'cliff-edge', the 'worst-case scenario', a 'no-deal Brexit', a 'WTO Brexit', an 'Australian-model Brexit' and a 'clean Brexit'. The range of terminology signifies to what extent the economic consequences of such an outcome are uncertain and hotly debated. To some it is an opportunity to take the brakes off the UK economy and build a new future as an independent global trading nation. To others it can only lead to a diminished future, with a shrinking economy and reduced international status and influence. There may, of course, be some sort of free trade deal, in which case the consequences can only be forecast once the outline of such a deal is known.

Business must be prepared for a no-deal Brexit, should it happen. Leaving aside concerns as to security, climate change and other political matters, and focusing on the economy, predictions of adverse consequences include an immediate recession, with increased unemployment. Paradoxically, there may also be labour shortages, since it is considered by many that British workers will be unwilling to fill the need for unskilled, low-paid manual work, principally in agriculture, but in other sectors as well, including fisheries. Labour shortages, in combination with trade barriers and tariffs, may disrupt supply chains and lead to a shortage of various types of goods. Significant currency fluctuations may push up inflation. In the 1970s, dire economic circumstances and a three-day working week led to power cuts, and it is not impossible that that could happen again.

Uncertain times

The striking thing is the extent to which the Covid-19 crisis has already brought, or seems likely to bring, some of those consequences. Travel restrictions, self-isolation and social distancing have all led to labour shortages, particularly in agriculture. With a predicted shortfall of 80,000 workers to help get the harvest in, the government suggested earlier this year that furloughed workers could be encouraged to help out. A 'Pick for Britain' campaign had 50,000 responses; however, only 6,000 completed the video interview, and only 112 have taken up jobs. This suggests that perhaps the unflattering stereotype of the British worker has something in it, and that filling labour shortages resulting from Brexit may be an uphill effort.

Disrupted supply chains and shortages of goods have been very much part and parcel of the Covid-19 experience, and while it remains to be seen what the economic consequences will be, recession, inflation and increased unemployment seem almost certain to be among them. It may be that if 'the worst' has already arrived, politicians will see no significant downside to a WTO Brexit.

There are other background pressures affecting particular sectors, too, which have been a feature of commercial life for a while, and which may give a clue as to some likely responses to the twin events of Covid-19 and Brexit.

Office market

Flexible office space has seen significant growth over recent years, and the trend shows no sign of slowing down. On one estimate, by 2030, 30% of all office space in the capital will be let under non-traditional, flexible leases. In part, the desire of office occupiers to retain agility and flexibility has been a signal of uncertainty over Brexit, but that one-off anxiety aside, the pace of technological change simultaneously enables and demands agility. Employee working patterns have shifted significantly, with IT infrastructure enabling home-working and hot-desking. The enforced mass experiment in adopting home-working technology as a result of Covid-19 is likely to accelerate this trend.

Business plans are increasingly drawn up for short periods: a year, or perhaps a quarter. In this context, commitment to a lengthy institutional lease is highly unattractive, particularly taking into account the impact of *International Financial Reporting Standard 16*, bringing lease commitments over 12 months onto an occupier's balance sheet.

A few years ago, serviced office suites were the principal solution, particularly for Small and Medium-sized Enterprises. Many new SMEs are in the financial technology, media, telecoms and creative sectors, which are particularly open to new thinking as regards office space, and which increasingly look to co-working solutions provided by the likes of WeWork and Workspace. Flexible arrangements encompass not only serviced space, but also co-working and so-called 'vertical campuses', in which occupiers may take one or more floors as core offices but also benefit from sharing centralised services and other facilities such as social space.

Larger corporates are also beginning to use flexible arrangements for their own occupancy, as well as seeing opportunities to offer flexible accommodation in surplus space to which they remain committed over a longer term. The big institutional landlords are increasingly ready to let space to co-working providers such as Workspace, and British Land has its own flexible working brand, Storey. WeWork experienced well-publicised difficulties at the end of 2019, but these seem to have arisen from management issues rather than from any lack of demand for flexible space.

Retail market

As regards the retail sector, the high street has been under pressure for a number of years. Major retailers entering into insolvency pro-cedures has become a regular feature of the press. High levels of vacancies of retail units are there for all to see. Much of this has been to do with the challenge from online retailing, of course. Retail Eco-nomics reported in 2019 that growth in online sales over the previous decade had been over 400%.

Figures published by the Valuation Office Agency for the year to 31 March 2019 indicated that 394,000 m^2 of retail space in England and Wales was lost in that year. To adopt the time-honoured measure, that is the equivalent of 55 football pitches. The figure relates to space which has been taken out of retail use permanently, rather than just space which is temporarily vacant. Those retailers who are successful have a much reduced appetite to take up space which has become available as other retailers have become insolvent, while landlords often decide to change the usage of vacant space rather than continue efforts to let it out to retailers.

Government has made efforts to help, with a one-year rates holiday from 1 April 2020 for businesses with premises of rateable value less than £51,000 – sectors benefiting being retail, leisure (including cinemas and music venues), and hospitality (including restaurants and hotels). The establishment of a £3.6bn Towns Fund was announced in the March 2020 Budget, to support the regeneration of high streets, town centres and local economies. In response to Covid-19, the one-year rates holiday has been extended so that there is no rateable value limit restricting its application. In addition, a business rates grant has been introduced, worth up to £25,000 for retail, hospitality and leisure businesses operating from smaller premises, with a rateable value up to £51,000. It is widely considered that the business rates scheme as it stood prior to the Covid-19 outbreak will not return, and that the crisis will force government to grasp the nettle of re-casting the tax, something for which pressure has been increasing for some time.

The impact of government action will necessarily be limited, however, and retailers and landlords must try to find new routes to sustained viability. Retailers have responded to pressure by trading in different ways, which require more flexible lease terms. They increasingly seek to share space with concessionaires or franchisees, sometimes irrespective of restrictions in the user clause, thus allowing the tenant to freshen up their offer by livening up the mix of occupiers. 'Experiential retailing' has become commonplace, with retailers offering classes in crafting, cookery and so forth.

Pop-up lettings have been a feature of the retail landscape for some years now, and have become mainstream. Christchurch, New Zealand, has a shopping mall comprised entirely of pop-ups, called Re:START. This came about with the aim of starting the regeneration of the city, after earthquakes destroyed existing shops. Shopping centre owners Westfield now dedicate space to pop-ups in all their centres worldwide, and they are used by luxury travel brand Kuoni and BMW (to promote its Mini brand), for example.

Some key issues

With this background, some key issues are apparent, which are as much issues of future lease drafting as they are of negotiating the crisis on the basis of existing lease terms:

- When faced with a public health crisis, or widespread closure of premises by tenants, what are the options for landlords? Can they close multi-let premises such as shopping centres or office complexes? Alternatively, can they reduce or suspend provision of services? The other side of the coin is: where such circumstances prompt landlords to additional expenditure on services, will the increase be recoverable from tenants?

- Can an event such as the Covid-19 pandemic or Brexit, leading a tenant to close its premises, relieve it of liability under the lease? In other words, what routes to lease termination will be open to tenants?

- What issues arise for tenants that have closed their premises, but whose leases remain on foot? There are practical issues of day-to-day management of the property, but also legal issues of continued liability in relation to lease covenants.

- For the landlord, what actions are still available, or effective, to enforce tenants' lease obligations?

- Where landlords wish to take an approach which is supportive rather than enforcement-based, what issues arise in relation to concessionary arrangements?

- Finally, how do these experiences influence the negotiation of leases in future?

These are the issues which will be addressed in the following chapters.

CHAPTER TWO
CLOSURE OF PREMISES BY LANDLORDS; SERVICES AND SERVICE CHARGES

Duties to tenants and the public

In the case of a single-let property, to which the landlord provides no services, it is hard to see any basis on which the landlord might have obligations to its tenant in relation to Covid-19. In multi-let properties, where the landlord provides services and acts as property manager, employing staff, there is potential for a different outcome, though in practice it will often be the same.

General health and safety duties imposed upon landlords (for example, in relation to legionella) rest upon the landlord having the requisite degree of control over the building to take action to control the risk. The transmission of Covid-19, though, will have no link to the construction, infrastructure or management of a building. Health and safety regulations are therefore unlikely to have much relevance.

The landlord may have duties to the public as regards the common parts under the *Occupiers' Liability Act 1957*, but provided they have taken all reasonable steps to ensure that visitors will be reasonably safe there should be no liability under this legislation. Compliance with the recommendations of Public Health England should be sufficient.

Complete or partial closure

Duty or not, landlords may conclude that specific developments should be closed entirely. That might be as a result of concerns over safety of staff, tenants and the public, or possibly because staff shortages as a result of Covid-19 make it impossible to run the development with the necessary services, or it might be that the occupancy level has fallen so low that keeping the development open is uneconomic. The latter situation might not be Covid-19-related; it could conceivably arise in some of the more lurid post-Brexit scenarios, where not only multiple tenant insolvencies, but also potentially labour shortages, even interruptions to power supply, could also prompt consideration of closure.

Force majeure clauses will receive consideration in the next chapter; for present purposes it is sufficient to note that it would be unusual to find a force majeure clause included in the leases within a development, permitting a landlord to close it. In any event it is far from clear that a force majeure clause would be triggered by present circumstances, or indeed Brexit. In the absence of any contractual right, closure would give tenants claims for derogation from grant, breach of quiet enjoyment, and potentially private nuisance, and might be considered to be a repudiatory breach, giving tenants opportunity to terminate their leases.

This is therefore a step which landlords will be very reluctant to take unilaterally, though it might prove possible to agree with all tenants that a development should be 'mothballed'. As regards Covid-19 and shopping centres, though, any centre is likely to contain some retailers on the 'essential' list, and therefore exempt from the general closure requirement, such as supermarkets, pharmacies and newsagents. Unanimous agreement in such a case would therefore be unlikely.

The writer is not aware of any instances of landlords closing developments in response to the Covid-19 pandemic. Perhaps more likely is that they may consider closing some or all of the common parts, if the layout of the development makes that possible while still preserving access for those tenants whose premises remain open. Most leases will provide for suspension of access to common parts in the event of an "emergency", and the Covid-19 pandemic could easily come within the intended meaning of that word. Certainly, the government's lockdown must be seen as an emergency measure. Also, landlords are generally entitled to implement reasonable regulations for the management of the building: existing regulations might permit suspension of access to some or all of the common parts; or new regulations might be made in response to the circumstances.

As lockdown measures are now beginning to be dismantled, these issues are likely to recede, for the present at least.

Services and service charges

Another possible response to crisis conditions is landlords limiting or suspending the provision of services. Service charge clauses often provide that the landlord must use "reasonable endeavours" to provide services, rather than imposing an absolute obligation. They will usually relieve landlords from liability for a failure to provide services if they are prevented from providing them for reasons beyond their control. So if all the reception staff are quarantined, for example, the tenants may not be in a position to complain about the landlord not providing a manned reception area. Again, while Covid-19 has given cause to consider this possibility, it is by no means impossible that the impact of Brexit will see landlords struggling to provide services.

If non-provision of services were to extend to matters such as cleaning of common parts, or weekly fire alarm tests, or provision of security, individual tenants would have to consider the health and safety implications for their staff.

Non-provision of services is one issue, but another is the exact opposite: landlords seeking to recover the cost of providing additional services. (That pill may be sweetened, to some extent at least, by a reduction in other elements of service charge as a result of landlords having closed common parts, or suspended or restricted services for a period). One source of additional costs arising out of Covid-19 has been landlords arranging for more frequent, thorough deep-cleaning of common parts, particularly surfaces which are touched regularly, such as handrails, door handles, lift buttons and toilets.

As always, the individual terms of the lease will need to be consulted, but it would be unusual to encounter a service charge provision which did not:

(a) Provide for the landlord to recover the costs of cleaning; and

(b) Allow the landlord to add to or vary the provision of services where "reasonable" or "in accordance with the principles of good estate management".

Most landlords will therefore start from a good position in seeking to establish that such costs are recoverable.

Additional costs may also arise as a result of the gradual dismantling of lockdown measures, as businesses within multi-let premises re-open. Tenants who are themselves having to grapple with social distancing requirements in their workspaces will have concerns over the areas of a building where they have no control, such as the lobbies, lifts and washrooms. The tenants themselves will be unable to exercise control over those areas, and will be reliant on measures taken by landlords and managing agents.

It will not in many cases be practical for commercial property land-lords to restrict entry to a building by having, for example, staff queuing outside, as we have seen with supermarkets, so as to limit the number of people in a building at any one time. Individual busi-nesses may be able to phase the time of staff arriving or departing, but this could prove impractical in large multi-let workspaces.

Realistically achievable solutions include requiring staff and visitors to wear face masks in common areas and increasing cleaning regimes, together with social distancing measures, such as restrictions on lift users, cutting the capacity of particular rooms by removing chairs, and signposting walking directions. Temperature screening, alloc-ating a separate isolation room for those with symptoms, disabling any touchscreens and removing any shared items which are fre-quently touched (like remote controls) are also options. Landlords may even wish to move to no/low-touch doors, switches and other fittings. Measures of this sort will also have a cost, and landlords will be looking at recovery of such costs via the service charge.

Again, landlords may be reliant upon so-called 'sweeper clauses' in service charge provisions. The *RICS Professional Statement on Service Charges in Commercial Property* sets out that such provisions should be used primarily where the length of term of the lease may mean that there is uncertainty in the nature of services which may be provided in the future: "*A sweeper clause cannot be used to cover the cost of something that was left out of the lease in error. The intention is to give the owner the ability to provide further services that are not iden-tified or in contemplation at the time the lease was granted, and that, for any reason, are considered necessary or desirable to be provided at a later time.*" That description seems very apt for present circumstances. Of course there may always be argument as to what is reasonable, and whether a landlord has exercised its discretion correctly.

Landlords will also need to bear in mind any restrictions to which they are subject as to hours during which servicing of their premises may take place, and this may require co-operation with tenants, neighbouring occupiers and planning authorities.

CHAPTER THREE
CLOSURES AND LEASE TERMINATION

Tenants whose premises are closed, whether voluntarily or compulsorily, are likely to be looking for legal justification for non-performance of lease obligations, principally of course payment of rent. They may therefore seek to establish that the lease has been terminated. Landlords will naturally resist this, not least because termination will leave the landlord with the liability for business rates, subject to any available reliefs.

Circumstances of extraordinary economic difficulty may result in multiple tenants falling into insolvency, in which case lease terminations are likely to follow anyway. Economic difficulty may follow from Covid-19 and the subsequent lockdown, or from Brexit, or from a combination of both. As regards tenants who avoid insolvency, there has been much commentary prompted by the Covid-19 episode about their other potential routes to lease termination, although the consensus is that such routes as there are will not often be available.

Contractual termination

The one guaranteed route to lease termination, of course, is any applicable contractual basis. This may simply be a matter of waiting for lease expiry: with shorter leases now being the norm, lettings of three years or less are not uncommon, so for certain tenants, the exposure to continued rental liability may not be too severe. This may apply particularly in the retail sector, where short lease terms have been most prevalent.

Retail tenants, too, have been looking in recent years for leases incorporating more frequent, simplified break rights, and there may be opportunities to terminate leases in this way.

For office tenants, flexible occupation terms (frequently licences of six months or less, with easy termination provisions) will often provide a ready escape route. The clue, as they say, is in the word 'flexible'. It has been reported that WeWork is now trading at 35% of its pre-pandemic level.

Force majeure

Another sort of contractual provision which may potentially be relevant is a force majeure clause, which will provide that in certain specified circumstances the parties can terminate the contract, or perhaps suspend or delay performance of obligations. Such provision is usually to be found in construction contracts, but is rare in modern leases, so it will be few tenants who have this escape route. Licence agreements in relation to serviced offices do sometimes contain force majeure clauses, and more historic leases may also contain them, and so leases and other occupational documents should be reviewed.

The presence of such a clause is not the end of the story, however, since everything will depend on its wording. Force majeure is often considered to be analogous to catastrophes or Acts of God that are beyond a party's control, such as earthquakes and typhoons, but also human disasters such as wars, terrorism and strikes. In some civil law jurisdictions, such as France, the term is defined, and relief prescribed, in the applicable civil code. In English law, on the other hand, force majeure is a creature of contract, so the availability and scope of force majeure relief will depend entirely on the terms of the relevant contract.

If the clause contains an exhaustive list of force majeure events, they must be considered to see if they might cover the applicable circumstances (the Covid-19 pandemic, or Brexit). While it is unlikely that leases will specifically list 'Covid-19' or 'coronavirus' in a force majeure definition, there may be other terms that will be applicable, such as 'pandemic' or 'epidemic'. If the list is non-exhaustive, or if there is a definition in more general terms, then there will likely be greater room for arguing that those circumstances are covered in principle. A definition of force majeure may be broad enough to cover governmental measures such as closure of premises, travel restrictions or quarantines.

Generally, though, force majeure clauses are interpreted strictly by the courts and may be regarded as operating only where performance has become physically or legally impossible, not merely more difficult or unprofitable (*Thames Valley Power v Total Gas & Power 2005 EWHC 2208 (Comm)*). Covid-19 or Brexit are more likely to be considered as events which hinder performance of the terms of a lease rather than preventing it altogether.

Frustration of lease

Any kind of contract, including a lease, may be terminated by frustration if an event occurs which makes it impossible to perform an obligation, or renders the obligation radically different from what was in the parties' contemplation at the time the contract was entered into. The principle is similar to force majeure, but does not rely upon express contractual provision.

There is some support in caselaw for the possibility of termination of a lease by frustration. In *National Carriers Ltd v Panalpina Northern Ltd [1981] AC 675*, the House of Lords accepted that in principle this was possible, while emphasising that the circumstances in which it might happen would be exceptional (the obliteration of the site of the property by a cliff collapse, perhaps). There was a recent unsuccessful attempt to establish that a lease had been frustrated by the United Kingdom's decision to leave the European Union, in *Canary Wharf (BP4) T1 Ltd v European Medicines Agency [2019] EWHC 335 (Ch)*, and it remains the case that there is no recorded instance of a frustration argument succeeding in relation to a lease.

The *Canary Wharf* case may well deter any further attempts to rely upon Brexit as a frustration event, though the terms of the final Brexit deal (or no-deal) potentially present a rather more concrete basis for arguing frustration than simply the referendum result.

The Covid-19 pandemic itself is not very convincing as a frustration event, since it does not render the enjoyment of possession of the demised premises impossible.

Temporary closure of premises by government order might be a different matter, though such authority as there is suggests that that too would probably not be regarded as making a sufficient alteration to the circumstances as to amount to frustration.

There was a case in *Hong Kong (Li Ching Wing v Xuan Yi Xiong [2003] HKDC 54)*, relating to the 2003 SARS outbreak, where a tenant tried to terminate his tenancy because the Department of Health issued an order isolating the premises for 10 days. The court held that a period of 10 days was relatively insignificant in the context of a two-year tenancy agreement and therefore the tenancy had not been frustrated.

A closure lasting even for some months, in the context of a five or ten-year lease, is unlikely to be considered a frustrating event. Perhaps there may be a better case for it where the remaining lease term is very short, and particularly if the closure will extend beyond expiry. However, any tenant that succeeds in establishing frustration of its lease will have made legal history.

Repudiatory breach by landlord

Where a landlord has closed multi-let premises, or is failing to perform obligations, such as provision of services, a tenant may have an argument for termination of its lease on the basis of repudiatory breach by the landlord. There have been occasional instances of a lease having been held to be terminated by the tenant's acceptance of a landlord's repudiatory breach.

- In *Hussein v Mehlman [1992] 32 EG 59*, a landlord of residential property which was let on an assured shorthold tenancy agreement was in breach of his repairing obligations, and the County Court concluded that that breach amounted to a repudiation of the tenancy agreement. The tenant vacated the property and returned the keys; in so doing, the court concluded, he had accepted the landlord's repudiation of the tenancy agreement, thereby terminating it.

- In *Chartered Trust plc v Davies (1998) 76 P&CR 396*, the Court of Appeal held that the landlord had repudiated the lease by its derogation from grant, and that the lease had been terminated by acceptance of that repudiation. The landlord in that case had failed to prevent a nuisance by a neighbouring tenant in the shopping mall. There was no argument as to the applicability of the doctrine of repudiation, however. It was simply accepted, and *Hussein v Mehlman* was not considered.

- Both cases were relied upon in the High Court in *Nynehead Developments Ltd v RH Fibreboard Containers Ltd [1999] 1 EGLR 7*, as authority for the applicability to leases of repudiation and acceptance. The landlord had failed to act effectively to control competition for parking on an industrial estate, but the claim failed on the facts, the court finding that the landlord's conduct did not amount to repudiation.

- In *Reichman v Beveridge [2006] EWCA Civ 1659*, where some doubt was expressed on the proposition, it was noted that there was no Court of Appeal authority in which the question, whether or not the doctrine of repudiation applied to leases, had been fully argued and ruled upon. It was unnecessary to decide the issue in that case.

- Most recently, in *Grange v Quinn [2013] 1 P&CR 18*, it was stated in the Court of Appeal that: "*it is now clear that a lease may be brought to an end by repudiation and acceptance ... In the present case the defendants' conduct in unlawfully and permanently evicting the claimant was a repudiation which necessarily brought the lease to an end without any need for acceptance.*" Again, though, this was without argument on the point, and the decision for the court in that case was not whether the lease had been terminated, by whatever means, but the assessment of damages for unlawful eviction.

The caselaw can fairly be said to be developing, but the landlord's breach would have to be fundamental in nature to justify termination on this basis: perhaps, denying access, or a total failure to provide services including the essentials of heating, lighting and water. This is speculation, though, and temporary measures in accordance with statutory requirements, or in response to a public health crisis, might not demonstrate the requisite intention on the landlord's part not to be bound by the lease. Landlords may be able to defend any such claims on the basis of an implied term, arguing that it was contemplated by both parties that if there were a major incident which involved a serious risk to health, the parties would take steps such as closing the premises.

Disclaimer

There is another way out for tenants, but it is very much dependent upon the commercial realities of the particular case. For this option to work, four conditions need to be satisfied:

(a) The tenant is a company, in occupation of only one leased property;

(b) The directors and shareholders are prepared to see the company liquidated;

(c) They are moreover willing and able to pay the landlord compensation; and

(d) No directors or shareholders have guaranteed performance of the tenant's obligations under the lease.

If all those conditions are satisfied, the company can enter into a members' voluntary winding-up; in other words, a solvent liquidation (assuming the tenant company to be solvent, of course). Once the liquidator has been appointed, it has power to disclaim the lease by serving notice under *s.178(2), Insolvency Act 1986.* Disclaimer terminates the lease, but does not terminate the liability of guarantors, hence condition (d).

Condition (a) is perhaps most likely to be satisfied either (i) in circumstances where the tenant is a subsidiary of a parent company, whose policy is to take each lease into a subsidiary incorporated for the specific property; or (ii) at the other end of the business spectrum, where the tenant is a small, one-site enterprise. In either situation it is highly likely that there will be either a parent company guarantee, or a director's guarantee, so that condition (d) will not be satisfied. The solution may not very often be available, therefore, but could be useful where it is.

Flexible office providers typically operate using a property-holding Special Purpose Vehicle as the tenant, which suggests that that might be a context in which this solution could work. The SPV is usually backed up by a parent company guarantee, which would point away from it, although in practice landlords may not find it all that easy to enforce against a parent company which is often overseas-based and relatively untested.

Where the lease is disclaimed in this way, the landlord can submit a proof of debt claiming compensation for the loss suffered because of the disclaimer, under *s.178(6)*. For the liquidation to remain a solvent one (potentially an important point for directors, especially those whose other directorships include publicly listed companies), the landlord's claim must be satisfied in full.

Of course, the amount can be disputed, as it was in *Re Park Air Services plc; Christopher Moran Holdings Ltd v Bairstow [1999] 1 All ER 673*. The landlord submitted a claim calculated largely upon the full rental for the property over the remaining lease term, totalling approximately £5.4m; the court held that the landlord was to be compensated, not for the loss of future rent itself, but for the loss of its *right* to future rent. Valuing that right required that an allowance be made for being able to re-let the property in future, and it was held there should also be a discount for accelerated receipt. The effect was to reduce the compensation to just over £1m.

The procedure effectively gives tenants a put option, requiring the landlord to take a surrender of the lease upon payment of a reverse premium. It comes with a price tag for the tenant, but that may be worth it, depending upon the circumstances.

CHAPTER FOUR
CLOSED PREMISES; LIABILITY FOR RENT AND OTHER TENANT'S OBLIGATIONS

Insurance

Covid-19 and the lockdown will naturally have turned tenants' thoughts in the direction of their business interruption policies, but most will have found that the cover is restricted to circumstances in which the business property has been damaged. AXA has published a bulletin stating that most insurances will not cover the consequences of a virus outbreak unless expressly mentioned in the policy.

It is possible (though comparatively unusual) for businesses to purchase an extension of cover for compulsory closure of the property in response to an outbreak of a 'notifiable disease', and Covid-19 was registered as such in England and Wales on 5 March 2020.

An instance of the difficulties faced by businesses is provided by Raymond Blanc. It has been reported in the popular press that following closure of 37 of his pubs and restaurants, cover has been denied on business interruption policies taken out with Hiscox. He maintains that cover included damages caused by contagious diseases, while Hiscox has responded that its policy wordings "do not provide cover for business interruption as a result of the general measures taken by the UK government in response to a pandemic". Proceedings are reported to have been issued.

Landlords will usually have loss of rent insurance, but this too is generally linked to physical damage to the property, and in any event pandemics are very unlikely to be included in the insured risks.

Everything will turn on the specific policy wording, of course.

Vacant property: notifications, and insurers' requirements

Where a tenant closes its premises for a significant period, it will often be required under its lease to notify the landlord of the fact. There is also usually a requirement under insurance policies to notify insurers, who may require various measures to be taken to secure the property. If this is not done, cover may be jeopardised. The usual trigger for these notification requirements is a 30-day period of vacancy.

Insurers' requirements may be fairly minimal for a low-value, low-risk property: draining the water system, sealing letterboxes and regular inspections. For substantial high-risk properties, they may include installing or upgrading physical measures such as locks, window-bars, CCTV and alarm systems, placing concrete blocks at the site perimeter to prevent vehicle access, and engaging a 24-hour security presence. The expense may be significant.

It was reported at the beginning of April that Direct Line, Allianz and AXA have amended the wording of commercial policies so that the period of vacancy before such requirements apply is extended from 30 days to either 60 or 90 days. Aqueous Underwriting and Zurich have gone further, waiving policy conditions in relation to unoccupied property completely.

That is no doubt helpful to tenants so far as it goes, and so long as it lasts, but whether insurers impose any requirements or not, a vacant property is always a security risk, and tenants who close their premises will need to consider what precautions are necessary.

Notices

Another issue for tenants is the monitoring of incoming post during any period of vacancy. Formal legal notices or court papers may be validly served at the property event though the tenant is not there, and not dealing with such items promptly may have serious consequences. This is particularly the case if the premises are also the tenant company's registered office address at Companies House, or the address for service given at the Land Registry for any property owned or leased by it.

Many property documents incorporate the service provisions of *s.196, Law of Property Act 1925*. This provides for various methods of service, including leaving the document at the demised premises. In *Blunden v Frogmore Investments [2002] EWCA Civ 573*, a notice was affixed to premises, but the premises had shortly prior to that been seriously damaged by terrorist action, and the security arrangements made it impossible for the tenant to see the notice. Since the landlord was aware of that, its behaviour was regarded as demonstrating bad faith, and the court held that the notice had not been validly served in accordance with *s.196*.

A landlord who knows that it will be impossible for the tenant to receive the notice if left at the demised premises may therefore fail to effect service. However, that probably will not apply to a landlord who knows that the tenant has closed its premises in response to Covid-19, since it will be quite possible for the tenant to collect post from the property.

Tenants should therefore arrange to collect mail, perhaps arrange also for the Post Office to redirect mail, and see whether the lease permits them to nominate a substitute address for service. Redirection of mail may take some weeks to come into effect, so tenants still need to be arranging to collect mail in the interim.

Break options

Where a break date is approaching, it may be assumed that a tenant which has closed its premises will want to exercise the break and terminate their liabilities under the lease. It is important, as ever, to pay attention to what conditionality attaches to the break. If the lease follows the *Code for Leasing Business Premises in England and Wales*, the conditions should be only (a) that the principal rent is paid up to date, and (b) that the tenant has given up occupation and there are no subsisting sub-leases. Compliance should present little problem in that case.

Many leases contain far more onerous break conditions, though. Problematic ones, for present purposes, include:

- Tenant to give up vacant possession. This is not simply a matter of going out of occupation, but may also require that chattels and tenant's fixtures have been removed.

- Repairing, decorating and reinstatement obligations have been complied with. The standard of compliance required is very high, and a condition of this sort may make it difficult if not impossible to operate the break in practice.

During the lockdown period, compliance with requirements of this sort may simply have been impossible, given travel and social distancing restrictions, and it is quite likely that break opportunities may have been lost. At present, travel restrictions do not prevent travelling for work purposes where the work cannot be carried out at home, and guidance has been issued for construction and similar contractors as to maintaining social distancing, so carrying out any required work to properties should not be impossible. There may be longer lead-in times, though, which tenants will need to take into account.

Other operational requirements

Closure of premises will not relieve tenants of the need to test fire alarms weekly, and depending on the nature of the premises and the business there will be other operational matters to consider. Occupiers whose business involves storing perishable goods on the premises, for example, will need to take steps to prevent or address rodent infestation.

Keep-open covenants

One very common lease obligation which can be problematic for retail tenants in the event of closure is the obligation to keep the premises open for trade during normal opening hours. Tenants should check how 'normal opening hours' is defined in the lease; there may be scope to agree with the landlord a variation to opening hours in response to extraordinary events.

If premises are closed by government action, tenants will point to the requirement in their lease to comply with statutory requirements. Trading in defiance of a government-directed closure could incur substantial penalties. It is widely considered that the statutory requirement covenant would trump the keep-open covenant, so that there would be no remedy against the tenant for breach of the latter in those circumstances.

In any case, keep-open covenants are notoriously difficult to enforce. The House of Lords case of *Co-operative Insurance Society Ltd v Argyll Stores (Holdings) Ltd [1998] AC 1* established that it is only in exceptional circumstances that such a covenant will be enforced by specific performance. Damages are in principle available, and significant damages have been recovered in some reported cases (e.g. *Transworld Land Co v J Sainsbury plc [1990] 2 EGLR 255*) though it is likely that loss in the sense of a wider impact upon the shopping centre as a whole will only be capable of being identified and quantified against an anchor tenant or major multiple, and not against smaller businesses. An obvious point is that if a tenant closes its premises because of serious financial difficulties, whether caused by Covid-19 or Brexit, the value of a damages claim against them will be questionable.

Liability for rent

Leases will mostly only provide for suspension of rent in the event that the premises are damaged or destroyed by an insured risk, and so will not assist tenants. Some leases do extend the application of such provisions to certain uninsured risks, though it is very unlikely that this will extend to Covid-19. An uninsured risk is usually defined as an insured risk against which cover ceases to be obtainable in the London insurance market on normal commercial terms and at normal commercial rates.

Even if Covid-19 were included by general wording, the limitation to circumstances where the risk has caused damage to the property means that such clauses are unlikely to provide a basis for the tenant to withhold payment of rent.

If a landlord has closed common parts, or ceased to supply services, that potentially gives rise to a damages claim by the tenant, which has potential to justify withholding rent. However, leases invariably provide that rent and other sums due under the lease are to be paid with no set-off or deduction of any kind. In any event, a tenant which has closed its premises may struggle to establish that it has suffered any loss as a result of landlord action of that kind.

Tenants will almost always, therefore, face continued liability for rent despite what might be an open-ended closure of the premises.

Traditional types of turnover rent arrangements are unlikely to assist retail tenants in this respect. Such arrangements usually incorporate a 'base rent', typically 75-80% of open-market rental value, payable regardless of whether the tenant is trading or not, plus a top-up element calculated upon the turnover generated by the tenant at the store. A tenant that is not trading is not generating turnover, and so tenants might hope to be able to pay the landlord only the base rent element. However, such leases usually entitle the landlord to sub-stitute a notional or deemed turnover when the tenant is not open for business, or sometimes to switch back to full open-market rent.

On the other hand, the growth of shorter, more flexible retail leases has seen an increasing use of turnover-only arrangements, where there is no base rent, and where there may be no ability to apply a notional or deemed turnover, or to switch to open-market rental. In such cases landlords face a total cut-off in rental receipts, while the tenant will reap the benefit of this ultimate rental flexibility – as intended.

Occupation for purposes of a business

Another issue raised by closure of premises is whether the tenant is thereby deprived of security of tenure under *Part II* of the *Landlord and Tenant Act 1954*. A tenant wanting to be relieved of its lease liabilities sooner rather than later may welcome that; on the other hand it may intend to re-occupy later, if its circumstances improve, or it may wish to preserve the possibility of a claim for compensation if it anticipates that the landlord will oppose renewal of its lease. In either case, losing the protection of the Act would be a serious matter.

The issue is the requirement, under *s.23* of the 1954 Act, that to qualify for security of tenure the tenant must be in occupation for the purposes of its business. In a situation where the tenant has closed its premises, it might be argued that it is out of occupation, and so, for example, a landlord might be in a position to serve a break notice, which would have its full common law effect of terminating the tenancy, and the 1954 Act would have no application. Or the tenant might still be out of occupation at the contractual expiry date, in which case, under *s.27(1A)*, the tenancy will terminate on that date, with no right to renew.

While this is potentially an issue for tenants to bear in mind, it is unlikely to present too much of a difficulty. First, a tenant that closes its premises but leaves behind all its goods, tenant's fixtures, equipment, communications infrastructure and so forth may well be regarded as not having gone out of occupation anyway. Occupation is a factual matter, to be judged upon the circumstances of each case.

Secondly the courts have developed, in cases such as *I & H Caplan Ltd v Caplan & Anor [1963] 2 All ER 930* and *Bacchiocchi v Academic Agency Ltd [1998] 3 EGLR* 157, the concept of the "thread of continuity" of business occupation, which may not be broken by temporary absences.

In the *Caplan* case, a landlord successfully opposed renewal of the lease, and the tenant vacated the premises. However, it appealed against the decision, and was ultimately successful, so that some five months later it was able to resume occupation and did so. The court held that the five months' absence had not broken the thread of continuity of business occupation, the tenant having at all times maintained an intention to re-occupy as and when able to do so; therefore, it had not lost security of tenure.

In the same way, a temporary absence due to Covid-19 and government-ordered closure of premises, or temporary financial difficulties, would probably not defeat renewal rights.

Rent review

Where rent review dates fall within the lockdown period (and there will no doubt have been many reviews falling due on the March 2020 quarter day), tenants will argue that their premises command a much reduced rental value compared to a few weeks previously. Of course, most rent review provisions are upward-only, and on that basis, regardless of any depressing effect upon rental values, there can be no reduction in the rent payable.

In any event, any depressing effect is likely to be temporary, which may mean that a hypothetical tenant, bidding to take the property for typically five or ten years, would take a longer view.

It is a commonly provided-for assumption upon rent review that the premises can lawfully be used for the permitted use. If the lease contains that assumption it will not be open to tenants to argue that the rent review should reflect the fact that retail and restaurant uses are currently unlawful. This will not prevent the rent review being impacted by the overall market sentiment, however.

CHAPTER FIVE
ENFORCEMENT OF LEASE OBLIGATIONS

The primary obligation of the tenant under a lease is the payment of rent, and of course severe economic disruption will threaten many tenants' ability to perform that obligation. In the Covid-19 crisis, for tenants who have been obliged to close their business premises, the economic disruption is direct and simple: they cannot generate income. Economic disruption of a more general nature appears inevitable in the period following the lifting of lockdown, and of course Brexit is considered by many to threaten more of the same.

Inclusive rents have become more popular in recent years; in such instances, if the tenant is not trading and unable to pay, the landlord is exposed to all of the property cost, including insurance, rates and property maintenance. Even under more traditional leases, where the tenant is required to pay not only rent, but also service charge, insurance premiums and business rates, as well as having repair obligations, there is every chance that a tenant who is not paying the rent will not be paying any of those items either. Many landlords are therefore left bearing all of the property cost, unfunded by their tenants.

Other breaches of lease covenants by tenants appear inevitable: keep-open covenants for retail tenants; repair covenants; potentially user and alienation covenants also, as desperate tenants offload their premises without too scrupulous a concern for obtaining landlord's consent beforehand.

Breach of covenant opens the tenant up to the various enforcement options available to landlords, although government has introduced a range of restrictions on such remedies. The restrictions are temporary in effect, and, at the time of writing, will all expire within the next few weeks. However, further action is likely, the applicability of the restrictions is expected to be extended, and it would not be surprising if some permanent changes were to be made. It could well be that the range of remedies to which landlords have been accustomed will not be fully restored by the time of Brexit and its aftermath.

Forfeiture for non-payment

Forfeiture of leases will not typically present many attractions to landlords, when difficult economic conditions prevail. The landlord would be taking on rates liability by forfeiting, and could have little confidence about re-letting until such time as the market recovers. On the other hand, forfeiture is conventionally regarded as the ultimate security for payment of rent, and is a quick, cheap and effective remedy against tenants who may find that they can, after all, manage to pay the sums due. In any event, the option is presently closed off by *s.82(1), Coronavirus Act 2020*.

s.82 provides for protection against forfeiture of leases, whether by peaceable re-entry or by court proceedings, for commercial tenants who are in default with payments of rent or other sums due under their leases. It applies to tenancies within *Part II, Landlord and Tenant Act 1954*, which (slightly counter-intuitively) includes contracted-out leases. It also applies to tenancies which would be within *Part II* if the lawful occupier were the tenant: in other words, where the tenant has lawfully parted with occupation, whether by subletting or otherwise. It does not apply to licences to occupy, or tenancies for six months or less (unless, in the latter case, the tenant has already accrued twelve months' continuous business occupation of the premises (*s.43(3), Landlord and Tenant Act 1954*)).

The right to forfeit for non-payment is suspended by *s.82(1)* during the initial period of the Act's application up to 30 June 2020, and any extension period. There are provisions (*s.82(4) to (10)*) in relation to pending forfeiture proceedings, and to existing orders for possession, which preserve the principle that there will be no evictions for non-payment during this period. The suspension applies to all sums due under leases, not just the principal rent.

However, *s.82(1)* does not erase the liability to pay, and where the landlord is entitled to charge interest under the lease on unpaid items, it will continue to accrue during the period. Also, *s.82(2)* provides that no conduct by or on behalf of the landlord during the relevant period is to be regarded as waiving the right to forfeit for non-payment of rent. The right will therefore remain unless explicitly waived in writing. (Landlords' conduct during this period may still waive a right to forfeit based on other breaches, though, so care is still required).

One potential outcome of non-payment of rent is that a landlord might attempt, upon lease expiry, to oppose renewal of the lease under the *Landlord and Tenant Act 1954*, on the grounds of persistent delay in paying rent (*s.30(1)(a)*). That has been anticipated, and is specifically provided for in *s.82(11)*, so that non-payment during the relevant period is to be disregarded for that purpose.

Even without that provision, any such opposition would probably fail; ground (a) was considered in *Hutchinson v Lambeth [1984] 1 EGLR 75*, and the court listed out some relevant factors which the court will take into account, including the reason for delayed payment of rent. In circumstances where a tenant has had difficulties in paying because of the impact of the Covid-19 pandemic, that could be expected to weigh heavily with the court. In order to uphold the landlord's opposition to the grant of a new lease, moreover, the court must consider that the nature of the tenant's default has been such that it "ought not" to be granted a new lease. That must be highly unlikely where the tenant's difficulties arise from Covid-19.

It should be noted that there is no requirement under *s.82(1)* to establish that non-payment is the result of the Covid-19 pandemic. The British Property Federation has reported that certain tenants are interpreting the measure as an instruction not to pay rent regardless of their circumstances, and since it extends to all payments under leases, it may mean that service charge, insurance premiums and other sums are also being withheld.

Estimates as to the impact of *s.82(1)* differ quite widely, but even the least gloomy suggest that only around 70% of commercial tenants have complied with their financial obligations during the pandemic – so far. At the other end of the range, it has been estimated by Knight Frank that only around 33% of retailers met their March quarterly rent obligations in full and on time. Intu has reported receiving only 29% of its quarterly rent roll, compared to 77% for the same quarter in 2019.

One can understand tenants taking advantage of *s.82(1)* by not paying the March quarter's rent, despite being able to do so, in anticipation of severe difficulties ensuing during the lockdown period. Those difficulties are now not anticipated but actual, and unless the period under *s.82(1)* is extended, tenants will shortly face paying two quarters' rent all at once. It seems likely that the June 2020 quarter day will be even more problematic than the March one, as cashflow problems for tenants and debt levels for landlords will be that much worse. Deferring payment creates a problem which will need to be tackled at some point and the sooner we know where the government is headed on this, the better for both landlords and tenants.

Forfeiture for other breaches

There is no equivalent suspension of the right to forfeit as regards any breach of covenant other than non-payment, so that landlords may perhaps exert pressure on tenants by focusing on matters such as disrepair. As well as exerting pressure to pay, landlords may have other motives, perhaps taking the crisis as an opportunity to 'shake the tree', and remove a few particularly unsatisfactory tenants. Given that many leases are now granted for terms shorter than seven years, and the *Leasehold Property (Repairs) Act 1938* has no application to such leases, there is no significant hurdle, at least in terms of substantive law, in the way of landlords pursuing forfeiture for breach of repairing obligation.

Hurdles there are, though, as a result of restrictions on proceedings in court. A landlord may issue forfeiture proceedings, but will then find it difficult to get much further, for the time being at least. *Practice Direction 51Z* was introduced into the *Civil Procedure Rules* on 27 March 2020, and has the effect of staying, for 90 days, all possession proceedings brought under *Part 55* of the CPR. It was originally to apply until 25 June 2020, but the period has recently been extended to 23 August 1990. It applies to both residential and commercial properties, and has the explicit objective of halting the progress of evictions during the pandemic. The Court of Appeal in *Arkin v Marshall [2020] EWCA Civ 620* made it clear that the stay would only be lifted in exceptional circumstances, such as where the stay was somehow promoting the spread of Covid-19.

Landlords have the option of forfeiting by peaceable re-entry, without recourse to a court, but this is usually effected by enforcement agents on the landlord's behalf, and social distancing and hygiene requirements make this problematic. The Civil Enforcement Agents Association, CIVEA, also the High Court Enforcement Officers Association, HCEOA, have suspended repossessions during the lockdown. Instructions to that effect were issued to county court bailiffs as well. As we emerge cautiously from lockdown, HCEOA has issued a best practice document, 'A Flexible and Sympathetic Approach to Enforcement', which indicates a limited resumption of efforts to enforce money judgments, but says nothing about repossessions. Similarly, CIVEA has issued a 'Post-lockdown Support Plan' indicating a phased return to activity, but this too is confined to money judgments.

A landlord might be bold enough to change the locks itself, without using enforcement agents. However, a tenant might then apply for an interim injunction to be restored to possession, which it would surely obtain, pending determination of an application for relief from forfeiture. The application for an interim injunction would be dealt with at the normal level of urgency, so far as possible, and *PD 51Z* would not apply to stay the application. The landlord might expect some disapprobation from the bench, if not costs penalties.

Forfeiture of leases, for whatever reason and by whatever method, has effectively been taken off the table for now.

In response to lobbying by tenants' groups such as ukactive (representing gyms and leisure centres), the government has introduced restrictions on other remedies as well. So far, the restrictions apply to monetary default. As regards non-monetary breaches, landlords are unrestricted in suing for damages, or seeking injunctive relief (unless the injunction is in substance a possession claim, in which case the stay under *PD 51Z* applies).

Commercial Rent Arrears Recovery

The use of Commercial Rent Arrears Recovery ('CRAR') is now, until 30 June 2020, available to landlords only where the tenant owes 90 days' rent or more. For a tenant paying monthly, that effectively means three months' arrears. In relation to the more usual quarterly basis, most quarters are about 90 days in length. As regards the forthcoming June quarter day, as the quarter is 97 days, the tenant could pay 8 days' rent, and be safe from CRAR. The September quarter is 87 days long, so if the restriction is extended that far, a tenant could leave that quarter's rent completely unpaid with no risk of CRAR. Even in the case of a tenant owing more than 90 days' rent, social distancing requirements mean that civil enforcement agents are only pursuing CRAR to the extent of chasing payment in correspondence, or perhaps personal attendance to arrange a payment plan. Removal and sale of tenant's goods is in practice not possible.

County Court debt claim

The landlord might sue in the County Court and obtain a money judgment which could potentially be enforced against the tenant's property. In practice, however, obtaining a hearing might not be easy, and in any event enforcement of debts is suspended for the time being.

Statutory demands/Winding-up

While statutory demands may presently be served, and winding-up petitions issued, since 23 March 2020 the Companies Court has been adjourning winding-up hearings for at least three months. The issue of a petition may have consequences for tenants in terms of credit ratings, and compliance with banking covenants, so there may still be value in issuing one, but at the same time as announcing the restrictions on CRAR the government also announced that legislation would be brought forward to void statutory demands and winding-up petitions served on commercial tenants unable to pay their bills due to coronavirus.

The likely form of that legislation can now be seen in the *Corporate Insolvency and Governance Bill*. At the time of writing it is currently working its way through the legislative process, and it may be on the statute book by the time of publication. In the meantime, the courts have already begun to restrain the presentation of petitions in anticipation of the change in the law (e.g. *Travelodge Hotels Ltd v Prime Aesthetics Ltd and others [2020] EWHC 1217 (Ch)*).

It is to be noted that the Bill is concerned with *corporate* insolvency only, so that statutory demands upon individual tenants, and bankruptcy petitions, are not restricted at all. As drafted, the Bill prevents creditors from presenting a winding-up petition to the court against a company on or after 27 April 2020 on the basis of a statutory demand served between 1 March and 30 June 2020. It therefore effectively neutralises a statutory demand served between those dates.

The restriction applies for the period 27 April 2020 to 30 June 2020 (or one month after the legislation comes into force, if later). Royal Assent is anticipated in mid- or late June, in which case the restrictions will have an initial expiry of mid- or late July. As with all the other temporary restrictions on remedies, there may be extensions.

As regards statutory demands served outside that period, a winding-up petition might still be presented, so long as the creditor can show reasonable grounds for believing either that Covid-19 has not had a financial effect on the company, or that the company would have been deemed unable to pay its debts, within the meaning of the *Insolvency Act 1986*, even if the coronavirus had not had a financial effect on the company.

It will be an unusual tenant that has not been affected financially by Covid-19, so that in practical terms it may be possible to wind up only those corporate tenants that were effectively insolvent before the pandemic.

Recourse against third parties

Where there are former tenants or guarantors on the lease, then recourse against them may be a useful option. Landlords will need to ensure that, as regards former tenants and their guarantors, they serve notices under *s.17, Landlord and Tenant (Covenants) Act 1995* as required, so that the ability to claim against them is not lost. It should not be forgotten that guarantors may seek to recover from the tenant pursuant to an implied common law indemnity, so this may ultimately not be sparing the tenant at all.

Equally, if there are sub-tenants, the landlord may serve notice on them under *s.81, Tribunals, Courts and Enforcement Act 2007*, diverting their rent to itself and away from the head-tenant. This a useful short-term fix, but again it simply increases the financial pressure on the head-tenant.

Further government activism?

Should the crisis extend for several months more, or in the event of a second spike in the pandemic, further restrictions might be thought necessary. More immediately, the June quarter day is looming, and almost all of the temporary restrictions on remedies outlined above are due to expire either shortly before or shortly afterwards, unless extended. An immediate unrestricted free-for-all, with landlords (and other creditors) racing to get in first to enforce payments, is unthinkable, so extensions of the various restrictions may be expected.

Code of practice

At the same time, government is naturally looking for more sustainable fixes, and the prospect of Brexit makes it all the more prudent to find ways of helping business in the medium- to long-term. There may be a sign of things to come in Australia, which has introduced a Mandatory Code of Conduct for commercial leases, as a response to the difficulties caused by Covid-19. Landlords and tenants are expected to negotiate co-operatively and in good faith to share the financial risk and cashflow impacts proportionately, and to be honest and transparent with each other.

As well as a moratorium on forfeiture, the Code provides that landlords must offer rent reductions which are 'proportionate' (assessed with reference to the extent of the tenant's loss of trade – potentially up to 100%). Interest cannot be charged for any rent that is waived or deferred; there will be a freeze on rent increases (except for turnover rents); and landlords cannot draw down from rent deposits, or enforce bank guarantees.

While the UK government's thinking may not be along exactly the same lines, it was announced on 29 May that government is working with certain businesses and trade associations (including British Chambers of Commerce, British Property Federation, British Retail Consortium and the RICS) to produce a code of practice of its own. The stated aim is to support high street businesses through the Covid-19 crisis by helping to guide and encourage all parties to work together, and providing clarity and reassurance over rent payments. No further detail is presently available, though it is apparently intended to benefit 'high street businesses and landlords' only, and therefore seems to be sector-specific. It will presumably not apply to, for example, industrial or office leases. The code is intended to be temporary and voluntary, though the government will explore options to make it mandatory if necessary.

Longer-term reforms?

Even if Covid-19 itself largely disappears in the UK within a relatively short time, the anticipated lengthy recovery from the economic consequences, coupled with apprehension over the impact of Brexit, may prompt the government to a critical examination of the range of remedies available to landlords more generally. (The following thoughts are those of the author, and do not reflect any ideas known to be under consideration at government level).

An obvious off-the-peg measure which the government could take would be to enact the Law Commission's proposed *Termination of Tenancies Bill*, abolishing the present law of forfeiture and replacing it with a new statutory code. That would be broadly welcomed by landlords as well as tenants, and would largely mitigate the harshness of the present law. If done promptly, it could effectively solve the issue of a sudden 'cliff-edge', with forfeiture suddenly becoming unrestricted, since the discretion afforded to the courts under the proposals would allow them to protect tenants as appropriate.

The government might also take the opportunity to legislate against upwards-only rent review. This was under consideration in the 1990s, though the government eventually drew back from taking that step, having been persuaded by the property industry that it presented too many complications. The alleged complications did not prevent legislation to that effect being enacted in Ireland, and it is an idea that might be revisited here.

Keep-open covenants might be outlawed or restricted, which in light of their limited usefulness in practice might not be too strongly resisted by landlords. The conditionality of break options could perhaps be addressed too, being a discrete area of law in which obvious injustices have disfigured the law reports over many years.

Those measures might be considered to be low-hanging fruit: not too controversial, popular with small business, and relatively easy to legislate for.

They would, though, represent the first few steps towards prescribing the form of leases, and a more radical approach might be to embrace that idea, and more generally to prescribe the content of, at least, shorter leases. The RICS and the BPF publish standard forms of short commercial lease, as does the Law Society, and they might form the basis for regulation. Inclusive rents might be made compulsory; even the introduction of rent control might not appear too dramatic, since it already exists under the *Landlord and Tenant Act 1954*.

All of this would represent a significant 're-set' of commercial property letting practices, but severe economic circumstances resulting from Covid-19, Brexit, or both, could be thought to present both the opportunity and the justification for that; particularly for a government which has the avowed intention to 'level up' disadvantaged regions and re-balance the economy.

CHAPTER SIX
RENT CONCESSIONS

We concluded the previous chapter by discussing longer-term measures that the government might take so that tenants should not face a sudden de-restriction of landlords' remedies. In many cases such measures might prove to be largely unnecessary, since the landlord and tenant relationship may already have been adjusted by means of a rental concession. Concession agreements are in wide use, in response to Covid-19, and the following are common types of concession which tenants are asking for:

- Deferment of rental liability

- A switch from quarterly to monthly payment

- A switch from payment in advance to payment in arrear

- A rent-free period

- A reduction in rent

- A reduction in service charge

- Draw-down from an existing deposit, rather than immediate payment of sums due. The draw-down might be used to pay outstanding rent and other sums, or sometimes to fund necessary repairs or other work.

- A switch to a turnover rental, or even a turnover-only rental.

While these concessions may in themselves be unwelcome to land-lords, a negotiation over a proposed concession also provides an opportunity for landlords to seek something in return: perhaps taking a break option out of a lease, settling a rent review, or extending the term. (One warning note, though: exacting a 'price' from the tenant may trigger liabilities for SDLT, VAT or corpor-ation tax, so the parties need to obtain advice on the tax consequences of any proposed concession).

Landlords may well want, in any event, to impose confidentiality terms, and perhaps to make any concession conditional upon the tenant pursuing any available government relief packages, with pro-vision for clawback upon receipt of bailout funds.

Just as was experienced in the wake of the 2008 financial crisis, there are potential knock-on implications of rent concessions which land-lords must be aware of.

Side letter or variation?

It will often be considered appropriate to document concessions by means of a 'side letter', rather than a formal deed of variation. This is usually because the intention is not to vary the lease, but only to effect a variation or concession which is personal to the parties. Landlords will invariably stipulate that any concession is a benefit to the specific tenant, and is not to extend to any assignee of the lease. They may need to consider also, where the concession is likely to last for some time, whether they are prepared for it to bind the landlord's successors in title. That may be important for the tenant, but can affect the value of the landlord's interest.

In drafting terms, a stipulation that the variation is personal to the tenant does not by itself deal with the issue whether a successor in title to the landlord will be bound in the event that the reversion is sold. When drafting a side letter, it is therefore important to address the point expressly.

If a side letter is silent on the point, it is quite likely that landlord's successors will take subject to it. The position differs slightly, depending upon whether the lease is an 'old' lease or a 'new' lease for the purposes of the *Landlord and Tenant (Covenants) Act 1995*.

'Old' leases

In *System Floors Ltd v Ruralpride Ltd [1995] 1 EGLR 48*, the Court of Appeal held that a side letter expressed as personal to the tenant (but silent as regards the landlord's successors) bound the successor to the reversion, even though that successor did not know of the side letter when it acquired the freehold. It was bound because the obligations in the side letter fell within *s.142, Law of Property Act 1925*, which provides that the burden of covenants that have 'reference to the subject matter of the lease' (i.e. touch and concern the land) automatically pass to any purchaser of the reversion. The test as to what covenants 'touch and concern' the land has been judicially recognised to be somewhat confused and unsatisfactory, but most lease covenants do, in practice.

For pre-1996 leases, it follows that landlord's successors will usually be bound, unless the side letter says otherwise.

'New' leases

s.142 does not apply to post-1995 leases. Instead, the 1995 Act provides as follows:

- a covenant includes a collateral agreement (*s.28*)

- a collateral agreement means an agreement collateral to the tenancy, whether made before or after the creation of the tenancy and regardless of whether it touches and concerns the land (*ss.2(1)* and *28(1)*)

- the benefit and burden of covenants are annexed to the relevant interest and will automatically pass to the assignee of the lease or the reversion (*s.3(1)*) unless the covenant is expressed to be personal (*s.3(6)*)

For new leases, therefore, variations contained in side letters will bind landlord's successors in title, unless expressly personal in nature, or unless the side letter provides otherwise.

Terms of deferment

If payment of rent is to be postponed, there must of course be a payment plan set out for the deferred amount. Where the deferment is to be paid by instalments, the landlord may wish to provide that non-payment of an instalment accelerates the remaining instalments.

The parties also need to agree what rate of interest (if any) should apply, and from what date. For instance, as regards a payment originally due on 25 March 2020, but now to be paid by (say) three instalments on certain specified dates, it might be stipulated that each of the instalments should include interest calculated on the instalment sum from 25th March, at the base rate; however, should the tenant default on an instalment, then the instalment sum should bear interest at (base rate + 4)% from the instalment date. That is an illustrative example only, and the parties might negotiate something different.

Extension of term

Many landlords are agreeing term extensions with their tenants as part of concession deals; for example, if the tenant seeks a six-month deferment of payment, the landlord may agree, but stipulate that six months be added on to the length of the term. The consequence of such an extension may be an implied surrender and regrant of the lease at common law, which raises issues for both landlord and tenant.

The circumstances in which lease variation might result in a surrender and regrant were fully considered in *Friends Provident Life Office v British Railways Board* [1995] 2 EGLR 55. Following assignment of a lease previously held by British Railways Board, the assignee agreed a number of variations to the lease, which were documented in a deed of variation entered into with the landlord. Some years later, the landlord sought to recover arrears of rent from British Railways Board, on the basis of their privity of contract liability. British Railways Board contended that the deed of variation had effected a surrender and regrant, and that they were therefore not liable to pay. The court held that they were, since the only instances of a lease variation which would necessitate an implied surrender and regrant were (a) extension of the term, and (b) extension of the demise, neither of which had been provided for in the deed of variation.

It is clear therefore that there will have been a surrender and regrant where the lease has been varied so as to extend the lease term. The consequences would include:

• Any guarantors, or former tenants and their guarantors, remaining liable on the lease prior to variation, would be released by the surrender.

- If the original lease was contracted out of the *Landlord and Tenant Act 1954*, that status would not apply to the new lease.

- The tenant would have a potential liability for Stamp Duty Land Tax on the grant of the new lease.

It might be that none of those consequences would matter in any specific case, but both landlord and tenant need to be satisfied of that. The way around the problem is to document the extension by means of a separate reversionary lease, though this too has potential SDLT implications for the tenant.

Payments covered

A concession might apply only to the annual rent, though tenants may argue for it to apply to service charge and other sums as well.

Service charges

Applying the concession to service charge is relatively easy to provide for in the unusual circumstance that the service charge is a fixed amount. However, in the more usual case of quarterly on-account payments with a year-end balancing exercise, the treatment of instalments and balancing charges may need some thought.

- If the concession is a straightforward payment holiday, it is just a matter of specifying whether the sums covered include any year-end balancing charge.

- In the case of a reduction in rent and service charge, where the quarterly payments are to be reduced by (say) 40%, the issue is whether the quarterly payment upon which the percentage is calculated is to be retrospectively adjusted once the year-end accounts have been prepared.

• Instalment arrangements may be more intricate. Say an instalment arrangement will extend beyond the service charge year-end. Assuming that a further payment becomes due as a result of the year-end adjustment, the amount might perhaps be divided by the number of the remaining instalments, and a corresponding amount added to each. Alternatively, or if all instalments fall due before the service charge year-end, the additional liability might simply increase the quarterly payments in the next year. The implications for calculation of interest would then need to be addressed.

Turnover rent

Similarly, in turnover-rent leases, a concessionary reduction may easily be applied to the base rent, but not so easily to any turnover element. Also, a landlord may wish to vary the formula for calculation of the turnover element following expiry of the concession, in the hope of recouping some of the loss through a later increase.

Rent review

If there is any approaching or pending rent review, the concession agreement needs to stipulate how any increase is affected by the concession, and whether the concession is to be disregarded upon review.

Impact on break options

Assuming that a tenant has a break option which is subject to conditions, including payment of the principal rent being up to date at the break date, the tenant will need clarity that compliance with the concessionary arrangement will satisfy any such condition.

Termination

Documentation of any concession must of course specify the duration of the arrangement. As well as specifying an expiry date, landlords may want to have the ability to terminate the concession in other events, such as tenant insolvency, breach of other covenants in the lease and so forth.

Consideration should be given to the consequences of early termination. Typically, the rent will revert to the original rate from that point on, though more aggressive terms might include back-dating the original rental over the previously-enjoyed concessionary period, together with payment of interest. A provision of the latter type was considered in *Vivienne Westwood Ltd v Conduit Street Developments Ltd [2017] EWHC 350 (Ch)*, and held to be an unenforceable penalty clause.

The law on penalties was changed by the Supreme Court in 2015 in the conjoined cases of *Cavendish Square Holding BV v Talal El Makdessi; ParkingEye Limited v Beavis [2015] UKSC 67*. The test now is whether the offending clause is a secondary obligation which imposes a detriment on the party in breach which is out of all proportion to any legitimate interest of the innocent party in the enforcement of the primary obligation.

The court held that the concession agreement in the *Vivienne Westwood* case, when read with the lease, created a primary obligation to pay rent at a reduced rate (and to observe the terms of the lease), with a secondary obligation to pay rent at a higher rate where the primary obligation was breached. The same secondary obligation applied whether a breach was one-off or repeated, minor or serious, and without regard to the nature of the obligation broken or any actual or likely consequences for the landlord. In the circumstances, the burden of the secondary obligation was out of all proportion to the landlord's legitimate interest in having the tenant comply with the primary obligation.

Landlords should attempt to find ways of ensuring that any penalty imposed in the event of default is proportionate to the impact of the breach.

Consent of guarantor and others

Landlords may require consent from a superior landlord, or from a lender, before entering into any concession arrangement. They will also need to ensure that any guarantors of the tenant's covenants in the lease are party to the concession agreement, since this is the only sure way of preventing the inadvertent release of their guarantee obligations pursuant to the rule in *Holme v Brunskill (1878) 3 QBD 495 (CA)*. That rule operates to release the guarantor from its obligations entirely, in the event of any variation in the tenant's obligations under the lease. It applies unless either:

- the guarantor consents to the variation; or

- the variation is patently insubstantial or incapable of adversely affecting the guarantor.

The court does not examine whether in fact there is any adverse impact upon the guarantor: it must be self-evident that that there is none. It might be thought, since the whole point of a rental concession is to reduce liability, not increase it, that that exception would apply, but there are hidden traps in concession agreements.

- The first is that landlords may seek to impose a modest management fee in relation to the costs involved in administering the concession. That extra fee could be enough of a detriment to engage the rule, and release the guarantor absolutely.

- The same applies to any additional interest provided for in a concession agreement.

- Stepped rent arrangements are another problem. Say a tenant pays rent at £10,000 per annum, but owing to present difficulties it persuades the landlord to agree that for the next three years it will pay £6,000 for year 1, £10,000 for year 2, and £14,000 for year 3. The total payable over the three years is £30,000, just as if the rent had remained payable at £10,000 per year. There appears to be no additional liability.

  However, should the tenant default in year 3, the landlord would be looking to the guarantor to pay at the rate of £14,000 per annum. Had the concession never been granted, default in year 3 would have led to a claim at the rate of £10,000 per annum, so the guarantor is exposed to a higher liability as a result of the variation. For the guarantor, that means a complete release from liability.

Rather than use mental energy (and client's money) on the point, the safe course is to insist upon the guarantor signing the concession agreement as well. It is common to see 'anti-discharge' provisions in a lease, whereby either the guarantor consents in advance to amendments in the lease, or the lease states that any variation made to it will not release the guarantor. These provisions are strictly construed in the guarantor's favour, and must be very clearly worded if the landlord's position is to be preserved. The safe rule is to obtain the guarantor's consent.

Lease renewals

If a concessionary arrangement is entered into with a tenant, and that concession is still in place at lease expiry, how might that affect the terms of any renewal lease? We are principally concerned with rent, and the amount of the rent in the new lease is determined in accordance with s.34 of the 1954 Act: the court is required to determine the rent at the open-market level, at the date of the hearing, and any previously agreed concessionary rental will not be relevant to that assessment. However, concession agreements may incorporate other matters, such as variation of the scope of the repair obligation, and in determining what the repair obligation should be in the new lease (indeed, all terms of the new lease other than the extent of the demise, length of term and rent) the court is required to apply s.35, not s.34.

The effect of s.35, as interpreted in *O'May v City of London Real Property Co Ltd [1983] 2 AC 726*, is that the terms of the old lease are taken as a starting-point; it may be difficult to move away from them. This raises the question whether the terms of the old lease, for that purpose, incorporate any continuing concessionary arrangement. There is no reported case in which the court has carried forward the terms of a personal concession into the terms of a renewal lease. The possibility was considered, though, in *Allied Dunbar Assurance Plc v Homebase Ltd [2002] EWHC Civ 666*.

The tenant in that case wished to underlet its premises, but could only do so by agreeing concessionary terms with the sub-tenant, which were contained in a side deed, expressed to be personal to the sub-tenant. The court considered that upon any renewal of the sub-lease, there was "*an **obvious risk** that the terms of the current tenancy will be held to be the terms which those parties have agreed should have effect as between themselves*" (emphasis supplied).

This is not a binding decision that concessionary terms *will* be carried forward upon renewal, but the fact that the Court of Appeal regarded it as an obvious risk should make landlords wary. They should try to ensure that any concession has expired or can be terminated before the lease is renewed.

CHAPTER SEVEN
IMPLICATIONS FOR
NEW LEASES

It was suggested in Chapter 5 that government might view the aftermath of the Covid-19 crisis, coinciding with the impact of Brexit, as a moment requiring a re-set of commercial letting practices; but whatever government may or may not eventually do, occupiers will certainly absorb the lessons of 2020 (and no doubt 2021), and re-evaluate their occupational requirements. In most sectors and most locations, the demand for commercial property is unlikely to outstrip supply to an extent that will enable landlords to resist pressure for change; they will have to accommodate their customers.

Length/flexibility of occupational terms

For the property world, perhaps the most discussed consequence of the Covid-19 experience has been what it might mean for the office market. For some, it has now been proved that home-working is effective, and popular with staff, and so the requirement for office space will diminish significantly. For others, being stuck at home has simply underlined the advantages of an office environment for socialising and establishing cohesive team identities, and perhaps even for the mental and emotional well-being of staff, so that the demand for office space should continue to be robust. Perhaps those managing office-based businesses will also be in two minds, and will be more inclined to seek maximum flexibility in their occupational arrangements, while the market finds its level.

In any event, for occupiers without the need to absorb initial outlay on expensive fit-out, or plant and equipment, ever shorter and more flexible accommodation terms are likely to be an important requirement. Retail and office occupiers will lead this trend, but food and beverage will feature too, with ever more pop-up outlets, and with shopping centres increasingly including 'food halls' in their offer, where a wide range of food outlets share cooking facilities and waiting staff, and diners eat in a shared seating area, around a central bar. Occupation terms for the food outlets are typically short and informal, often on licences to occupy. This sort of arrangement is likely to be increasingly in demand.

Occupiers are likely to seek more frequent opportunities to break their leases, on terms which do not include onerous and difficult-to-satisfy conditions. Landlords have traditionally been resistant to this trend, but may now be prepared to take the view that such arrangements offer a higher degree of predictability in relation to vacancies, and perhaps the chance to replace a struggling retailer with a more successful tenant.

There have been suggestions of incorporating rights to break which could be triggered in the event of government-mandated closure of premises, or a no-deal Brexit, but such clauses are being resisted by landlords quite robustly so far. They present problems of definition in any event, and a better way of offering some protection to a tenant may perhaps be to extend rent suspension provisions so that they apply in the event of government-directed closures.

Rent arrangements

Alternative rent arrangements are increasingly being tried. An increased shift to turnover rents, in retail, leisure and food and beverage, is an obvious likelihood. Moreover, with short pop-up lettings, landlords will increasingly be prepared to look at turnover-only rents, rather than the traditional model of a base rent with a turnover-based top-up.

Another rental structure which has also become more popular as leases have evolved, and which is not confined to retail and leisure, is the inclusive rent. That is, the tenant pays a flat rate, while the landlord bears the risk of fluctuations in the cost of insurance, rates and property maintenance. This is, of course, the antithesis of the familiar FRI or 'clear' lease, and many landlords will still not be prepared to grant leases on this basis. However, such ideas are not eccentric or left-field, but are reflected in, for example, the RICS' Small Business Retail Lease, and the BPF's Short-Term Commercial Lease.

Standard lease terms

The terms of those standard leases, and others available on the internet, may be something that landlords are increasingly prepared to adopt, although as just remarked, they are quite a departure from the traditional model. Whether such terms are acceptable to landlords will be circumstance-dependent.

In the case of premises within an ageing office development in a poor location, for example, landlords may be unable to let except on a short-term, and subject to a schedule of condition. If, in the course of a term of three years or shorter, significant work to common parts is required, such as replacement of a flat roof, a court will take some persuading that the parties intended the tenant to have to contribute to such a major cost, on the basis of such a limited interest (*Scottish Mutual v Jardine Public Relations (1999) EGCS 43*).

Trying to recover that cost, or trying to enforce repair liability at lease-end, involves significant expenditure upon professional fees, and at the end of the day such financial settlement as the landlord receives is often not spent upon repairing the premises. That outcome can be avoided by simply omitting to place those obligations upon the tenant, as in some of these standard lease forms.

Another driver to adopt such forms is simply the need to keep transaction costs down, when the turnover of tenants may be expected to be high.

Rent review

In the case of lease terms of sufficient length to justify the inclusion of a rent review, tenants will surely renew efforts to move away from the upward-only model. The courts have proved themselves willing to impose either-way rent reviews upon lease renewal, in *Boots the Chemist v Pinkland Ltd [1992] 2 EGLR 98*, and more recently in *Dukeminster Ltd v West End Investments (Cowell Group) Ltd (Central London County Court, November 2018)*. Despite this, it has been one aspect of leasing practice which landlords have defended very robustly and successfully, and they are likely to continue to be robust even in the face of increased pressure from tenants faced with significant uncertainties.

User, alterations and alienation

The growth in 'experiential' retailing, offering customers not only the opportunity to shop, but also to enjoy experiences such as craft workshops, escape rooms and boutique cinemas, is a challenge to traditional user clauses. However, experiences of this sort are something which online retail cannot offer, and so are increasingly valuable to bricks-and-mortar retail. For landlords, flexibility in use restrictions to allow this sort of offering gives the tenants a chance to create an increasing variety of reasons for customers to visit a scheme.

In the same way, leases might traditionally have prohibited public gatherings or overnight stays. Now, overnight stays have been offered by John Lewis, for example, as a means for customers to experience products, and public demonstrations of products, lifestyle classes, etc., may all be means to attract customers to retail centres.

Advertising has always been an important part of retailing, but now the speed and range of social media reaction means that it needs to be more responsive than ever. In that context, tight lease controls on signage or public displays can restrict tenants' ability to undertake timely marketing campaigns to capture a trend at the right time.

User and alterations clauses are likely to have to be more flexible than ever before, and the same may be true of alienation clauses. Retail occupiers need greater freedom to share space with concession-aires or franchisees; and office users may want to have the ability to offer space-sharing and co-working arrangements, in the event that they find themselves with surplus space.

Keep-open covenants

The fact that keep-open covenants are of relatively little worth to landlords, and do not pose much of a threat to tenants, may suggest that they will not be high on the shopping list of terms that parties will wish to move away from. However, breach of keep-open cov-enant does entitle the landlord to forfeit (as happened recently in *SHB Realisations Ltd v Cribbs Mall Nominees [2019] Lexis Citation 32*), so tenants may wish to resist keep-open covenants in more uncertain times. More major occupiers, too, will find the potential exposure to a damages claim unwelcome.

The tenant remaining open for trade is especially important to landlords in the case of turnover-rent leases, but even there the ability to substitute a notional or deemed turnover figure, or to revert to open-market rent, provides a better protection than the keep-open clause.

It has been suggested that there could be a carve-out from keep-open obligations in the event of government-directed closure, and that looks like an uncontroversial compromise.

Quiet enjoyment

As a quid pro quo for concessions on keep-open covenants, landlords might seek similar carve-outs from their quiet enjoyment covenants. Potentially such a carve-out might be drafted to apply more widely, perhaps if closures of lettable space within the development should exceed a certain percentage.

Services

Again, landlords' obligation to supply services might be subject to a similar cut-off point, or perhaps restricted to specified core services, such as heating, lighting and security.

Experience of attempting to recover the costs of additional services provided in response to the extraordinary circumstances of 2020 may leave landlords reluctant to rely upon sweeper clauses in service charge provisions. It may be expected that some attention will be given to specific heads of expenditure, to reduce uncertainty in future.

Service of notices

Finally, notice provisions might be brought up to date to permit service by electronic means, to avoid problems for both landlord and tenant.

. . . .

It was suggested in Chapter 5 that government may venture upon some regulation of commercial lease terms, and that some of the issues touched on in this chapter might be dealt with in that way. If not, then of course market forces and negotiating position will regulate matters as usual. The least likely outcome is that the clock will wind back to December 2019, and that there will be no change.

MORE BOOKS BY
LAW BRIEF PUBLISHING

A selection of our other titles available now:-

'A Practical Guide to the General Data Protection Regulation (GDPR) – 2nd Edition' by Keith Markham
'Ellis on Credit Hire – Sixth Edition' by Aidan Ellis & Tim Kevan
'A Practical Guide to Working with Litigants in Person and McKenzie Friends in Family Cases' by Stuart Barlow
'Protecting Unregistered Brands: A Practical Guide to the Law of Passing Off' by Lorna Brazell
'A Practical Guide to Secondary Liability and Joint Enterprise Post-Jogee' by Joanne Cecil & James Mehigan
'A Practical Guide to the Pre-Action RTA Claims Protocol for Personal Injury Lawyers' by Antonia Ford
'A Practical Guide to Neighbour Disputes and the Law' by Alexander Walsh
'A Practical Guide to Forfeiture of Leases' by Mark Shelton
'A Practical Guide to Coercive Control for Legal Practitioners and Victims' by Rachel Horman
'A Practical Guide to Rights Over Airspace and Subsoil' by Daniel Gatty
'Tackling Disclosure in the Criminal Courts – A Practitioner's Guide' by Narita Bahra QC & Don Ramble
'A Practical Guide to the Law of Driverless Cars – Second Edition' by Alex Glassbrook, Emma Northey & Scarlett Milligan
'A Practical Guide to TOLATA Claims' by Greg Williams
'Artificial Intelligence – The Practical Legal Issues' by John Buyers
'A Practical Guide to the Law of Prescription in Scotland' by Andrew Foyle
'A Practical Guide to the Construction and Rectification of Wills and Trust Instruments' by Edward Hewitt
'A Practical Guide to the Law of Bullying and Harassment in the Workplace' by Philip Hyland

'A Practical Guide to Dog Law for Owners and Others' by Andrea Pitt
'RTA Allegations of Fraud in a Post-Jackson Era: The Handbook – 2nd Edition' by Andrew Mckie
'RTA Personal Injury Claims: A Practical Guide Post-Jackson' by Andrew Mckie
'On Experts: CPR35 for Lawyers and Experts' by David Boyle
'An Introduction to Personal Injury Law' by David Boyle
'A Practical Guide to Claims Arising From Accidents Abroad and Travel Claims' by Andrew Mckie & Ian Skeate
'A Practical Guide to Chronic Pain Claims' by Pankaj Madan
'A Practical Guide to Claims Arising from Fatal Accidents' by James Patience
'A Practical Approach to Clinical Negligence Post-Jackson' by Geoffrey Simpson-Scott
'Employers' Liability Claims: A Practical Guide Post-Jackson' by Andrew Mckie
'A Practical Guide to Subtle Brain Injury Claims' by Pankaj Madan
'A Practical Guide to Costs in Personal Injury Cases' by Matthew Hoe
'The No Nonsense Solicitors' Practice: A Guide To Running Your Firm' by Bettina Brueggemann
'The Queen's Counsel Lawyer's Omnibus: 20 Years of Cartoons from The Times 1993-2013' by Alex Steuart Williams

These books and more are available to order online direct from the publisher at www.lawbriefpublishing.com, where you can also read free sample chapters. For any queries, contact us on 0844 587 2383 or mail@lawbriefpublishing.com.

Our books are also usually in stock at www.amazon.co.uk with free next day delivery for Prime members, and at good legal bookshops such as Wildy & Sons.

We are regularly launching new books in our series of practical day-to-day practitioners' guides. Visit our website and join our free newsletter to be kept informed and to receive special offers, free chapters, etc.

You can also follow us on Twitter at www.twitter.com/lawbriefpub.

Lightning Source UK Ltd.
Milton Keynes UK
UKHW020635140720
366504UK00004B/88